The World of HORSES
FRIESIANS

Lorijo Metz

PowerKiDS press™
New York

To Tiana and to Mattias, the Friesian stallion who taught her there is
no impossibility in life if you act with love in your heart

Published in 2013 by The Rosen Publishing Group, Inc.
29 East 21st Street, New York, NY 10010

Editor: Amelie von Zumbusch
Book Design: Kate Laczynski

Photo Credits: Back cover graphic (big horseshoe) © iStockphoto.com/Deborah Cheramie; back cover graphic (background horseshoes) Purematterian/Shutterstock.com; cover, p. 11 Alexia Khruscheva/Shutterstock.com; pp. 4–5 Olga_i/Shutterstock.com; p. 6 © iStockphoto.com/AntoinetteW; p. 7 (top) Julia Remezova/Shutterstock.com; pp. 7 (bottom), 16 iStockphoto/Thinkstock; pp. 8, 18 by Violet Tally from Fire & Earth photography; p. 9 Zuzule/Shutterstock.com; p. 10 © NaturePL/SuperStock; pp. 12–13, 20 © Animals Animals/SuperStock; p. 14 PHB.cz (Richard Semik)/Shutterstock.com; pp. 15 (top), 22 Mariait/Shutterstock.com; p. 15 (bottom) Peter Zijlstra/Shutterstock.com; p. 17 Nastenok/Shutterstock.com; p. 19 Dennis Donohue/Shutterstock.com; p. 21 Image provided by Bonnie View Farm, Alberta, Canada.

Library of Congress Cataloging-in-Publication Data

Metz, Lorijo.
 Friesians / by Lorijo Metz. — 1st ed.
     p. cm. — (The world of horses)
 Includes index.
 ISBN 978-1-4488-7431-6 (library binding) — ISBN 978-1-4488-7504-7 (pbk.) —
 ISBN 978-1-4488-7578-8 (6-pack)
 1. Friesian horse—Juvenile literature. I. Title.

 SF293.F9M48 2013
 636.1'3—dc23

                          2011052883

Manufactured in China

CPSIA Compliance Information: Batch #WKTS12PK: For Further Information contact Rosen Publishing, New York, New York at 1-800-237-9932

Contents

The Friesian

Whether they are riding onto a battlefield or into the center ring at a circus, Friesian horses are a beautiful sight. Their shiny, black coats and long, flowing manes make these horses stand out.

> Though Friesians have been around for thousands of years, they did not become popular in North America until the 1970s.

Friesians are one of Europe's oldest **breeds**, or types, of horses. In recent years, they have become popular in movies. After all, moviemakers love beauty and Friesians are beautiful!

Friesians are one of the few breeds of horses that are native to the Netherlands. These horses were once in danger of dying out. However, there are now more than 45,000 Friesians worldwide.

Black Beauties

People measure horses in hands. One hand equals 4 inches (10 cm). Most Friesians stand 15 to 17 hands from the ground to the tops of their **withers**, or shoulders. When they are full grown, they weigh about 1,300 pounds (590 kg).

Almost all Friesians are black. They have large, bright eyes and small ears that lean inward. Some have small white spots, called stars, between their eyes.

Like other horses, Friesians have clear vision, sharp hearing, and a great sense of smell.

Some Friesians, such as this one, have wavy manes and tails.

Friesians have long hair, known as feathers, on the backs of their legs.

The things that make Friesians stand out in a crowd the most are their long, silky manes and tails. These sometimes grow so long that they touch the ground!

Friesians are light draft horses. Draft horses are big, strong horses that are often used for pulling wagons and other heavy work. Friesians have the sturdy bodies and wide backs of draft horses. They also have the long legs and the high-stepping **gait**, or walk, of lighter horses.

Friesians hold their long, curved necks high. This gives them a proud look. However, they are

Though they are big, powerful animals, Friesians are gentle.

gentle and trusting around people. Friesians are smart and easy to work with. People train them for everything from pleasure and trail riding to some of the most advanced **equestrian**, or horse, events.

Caring for Friesians

Friesians need daily exercise and fresh air. They need housing, such as a barn or stable. Friesians eat hay and grains, such as oats and barley. They also need plenty of fresh water and a block of salt to lick.

A person called a trainer can teach your Friesian how to work with people and do the movements that are used in horse shows.

Friesians will graze, or eat grass, if they are kept in a grassy field.

A Friesian's long, silky mane and tail need special care. Owners often braid them to keep them clean and prevent tangling. Hair conditioner helps loosen knots before combing. At least once a year, an animal doctor called a **veterinarian** should visit your Friesian. A person called a **farrier** should look after the horse's hooves and trim them when needed.

Friesian Foals

Friesian mothers carry their babies, called foals, for 11 months. Newborns weigh between 75 and 100 pounds (34–45 kg). Hours after they are born, foals are running.

Foals stay with their mothers for about the first six months of their lives. Friesians **mature**, or grow, more slowly than breeds such as

As all foals do, Friesian foals drink their mothers' milk.

Thoroughbreds and quarter horses. Training under saddle, or with riders, does not begin until Friesians are at least three years old. Early training, called groundwork, prepares them to carry the extra weight of riders and gear. It also helps them get used to working with people. Friesians live between 25 and 35 years.

13

Friesland is famous for its black and white cows, which are also known as Friesians.

Friesians take their name from Friesland, which is a part of the Netherlands. People began **breeding** horses there over 2,000 years ago. The first Friesians were big, strong horses that were used for heavy work. However, the breed

has changed over time. In the sixteenth century, people bred Friesians with lighter, faster Andalusian horses from Spain. The horses that resulted were strong enough that they could carry riders and their heavy weapons. However, they could still move quickly across a battlefield. Over the centuries, Friesians have worked on farms, raced in trotting races, and pulled the carriages of kings.

Saving the Friesians

Years ago, people began breeding Friesians with other horse breeds. By the late nineteenth century, there were almost no **purebreds**, or Friesians that were not mixed with other breeds. In 1897, a group of people in the Netherlands decided to save the Friesians. They started a studbook for the Friesian

One reason Friesians nearly died out is because people stopped using them on farms. Machines took over many of the farm jobs that horses once did.

horse. The studbook was a way to **register**, or keep track of, Friesians.

Today there are studbook groups in Europe and North America. These groups also set rules for breeding, such as how big a breeding Friesian may be. They also say what color breeding Friesians must be and what markings they can have.

17

Riding Friesians

Horses wear different saddles for different styles of riding. This horse is wearing a dressage saddle.

Along with their strength and ability to move quickly and easily, Friesians are smart and love working with people. This make them perfect for the equestrian sport of **dressage**. Horses and riders train for years to master the advanced, dance-like movements of dressage. At dressage events, horses and their riders compete against each other. Friesians compete at all levels of dressage. This includes upper-level movements like the **piaffe**, in which horses trot in place.

People also train Friesians for other styles of riding, such as pleasure and trail riding. With their good looks and fancy, high-stepping trot, Friesians are also popular in circus acts.

This Friesian is getting ready to take part in a dressage competition.

19

Carriage Horses

Their strength and beauty make Friesians popular carriage horses. In driving competitions, Friesians compete at pulling carriages with different-size teams. In tandem driving, two horses pull a carriage. They walk one in front of the other. Horses in driving competitions also compete alone and in groups of four.

This team of Friesians is taking part in a pleasure-driving competition.

This Friesian is pulling a sjee. "Sjee" is the singular form of "sjezen."

In the Netherlands, you can still see Friesians pulling small, wooden carriages called **sjezen**. At Friesian horse shows, one of the last events is often the quadrille. In this event, eight sjezen pulled by Friesians take the stage. A man and a woman who are dressed in nineteenth-century costumes drive each carriage.

In recent years, Friesians have become more popular worldwide. This is due in part to their appearance in movies. In 1985, the Friesian horse Othello appeared in the movie *Ladyhawke*. Since then, Friesians have appeared in many movies.

People who own Friesians know that they have more to offer than just their strength and beauty. They are also kind, gentle horses. This ancient breed of horse is sure to be around for years to come.

Glossary

breeding (BREED-ing) Bringing a male and a female animal together so they will have babies.

breeds (BREEDZ) Groups of animals that look alike and have the same relatives.

dressage (dreh-SAZH) Dance-like movements that horses are trained to do.

equestrian (ih-KWES-tree-un) Having to do with riding horses.

farrier (FER-ee-er) A person who puts shoes on horses.

gait (GAYT) Way of walking.

mature (muh-TOOR) To grow.

piaffe (pee-AF) A dressage move in which a horse trots without moving forward.

purebreds (PYUHR-bredz) Animals that are of only one breed.

register (REH-jih-ster) To record officially.

sjezen (SHAY-zun) Small, fancy carriages from the Netherlands that are pulled by horses.

veterinarian (veh-tuh-ruh-NER-ee-un) A doctor who treats animals.

withers (WIH-therz) A place between the shoulders of a dog or horse.

Index

Websites

Due to the changing nature of Internet links, PowerKids Press has developed an online list of websites related to the subject of this book. This site is updated regularly. Please use this link to access the list: www.powerkidslinks.com/woh/frie/